START-UP
CITIZENSHIP

IMPROVING OUR SCHOOL GROUNDS

Louise and Richard Spilsbury

Evans

Published by Evans Brothers Limited
2A Portman Mansions
Chiltern Street
London W1U 6NR

© Evans Brothers Limited 2007

Produced for Evans Brothers Limited by
White-Thomson Publishing Ltd.
Bridgewater Business Centre, 210 High Street,
Lewes, East Sussex BN7 2NH

Printed in China by WKT Co. Ltd.

Editor: Clare Collinson
Consultant: Roy Honeybone, Consultant in Citizenship
Education and Editor of *Teaching Citizenship*, the
journal of the Association for Citizenship Teaching
Designer: Leishman Design

British Library Cataloguing in Publication Data
Spilsbury, Louise
    Improving our school grounds - (Start-up citizenship)
    1. Playgrounds - Design - Juvenile literature
    2. Citizenship - Juvenile literature 3. School
    environment - Juvenile literature
    I. Title II. Spilsbury, Richard, 1963-
    371.6'1

ISBN-13: 978 0 237 53267 3

Acknowledgements:
Special thanks to the following for their help and
involvement in the preparation of this book: staff, pupils
and parents at Holyoakes First School, Redditch and
Matchborough First School, Redditch; Learning
Through Landscapes.

Picture Acknowledgements:
Alamy pp. 4 (left), 18 (right) (Jeff Morgan), 19 (Jeff
Morgan); Martyn Chillmaid pp. 4 (right), 6, 9 (left), 10
(both), 11, 14, 15 (both), 18 (left), 21; Corbis p. 16
(John Walmsley); Learning Through Landscapes pp. 1, 5
(both), 8 (both), 9 (right), 12 (both), 13, 20 (both);
Topfoto/ImageWorks cover.

Artwork:
Emily Manolopoulos p. 17; Hattie Spilsbury p. 7.

Contents

In the school grounds

What happens in your school grounds?

▲ Sam and his friends often play chase at playtimes.

► In the summer term, Sally and her friends stay after school for a netball club in their school grounds.

play   playtimes   club

► In this playground children sit on the **friendship bench** if they are **lonely** at playtime.

"When I sit here people come and talk to me."

◄ This garden area is used for **science** lessons. These children are using nets to see what minibeasts live in the school pond.

What do you like doing in your school grounds?

friendship bench   lonely   science

Improving playtime

What **features** of your school grounds make playtime fun? What do you **dislike** about your school grounds?

"There is nothing to play with in our playground. Sometimes we get bored and argue."

What **changes** would **improve** playtimes for you and your friends?

features   dislike   changes   improve

Which parts of your school grounds are used for different **activities**? Where can you run, sit or play football?

► Sunita drew a map of her school grounds. She used face **symbols** to show the places that make her happy and the places she dislikes. Which are her **favourite** places?

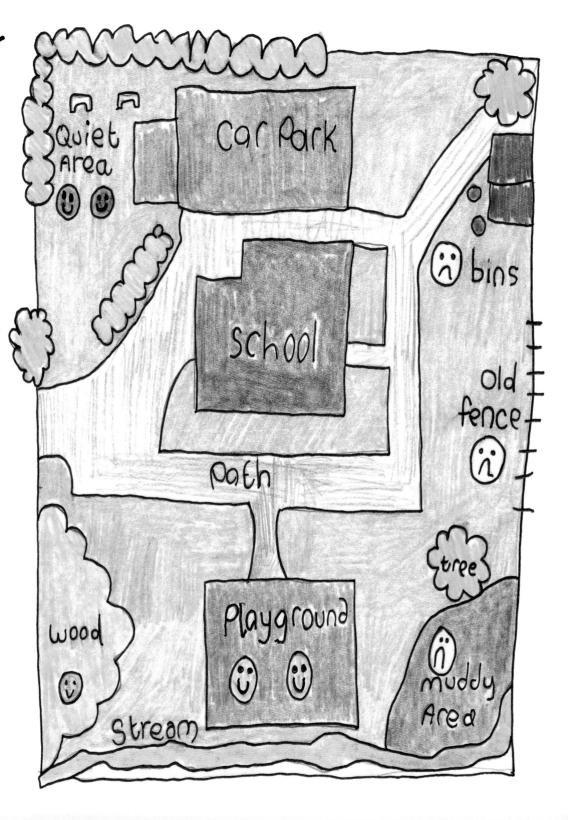

activities   symbols   favourite   **7**

Smarten up!

Dan's class decided to improve their school grounds. The children asked parents and friends to help.

▲ A new fence was put up. Dan and his dad helped to paint it.

▲ An artist helped the children paint a mural. Can you guess what the children are saying in the mural?

artist   mural

Litter makes school grounds dirty and ugly. Whose **responsibility** is it to keep the school grounds tidy?

▲ Holly is **recording** where people leave litter. Her friends take notes. Why do you think there is litter by this bench?

► Holly and her friends **design** a bright pattern for a litter bin. Do you think this will help to reduce litter?

responsibility   recording   design

Taking surveys

What do different people think of your school grounds? What **improvements** would parents, teachers and older pupils like to see? Who else would you ask?

"I would like a garden area where my class can study plants and minibeasts."

"I'd like a quiet place to sit and talk with my friends."

Why is it important to find out other people's opinions?

improvements   opinions

► Neela and her friends do a survey. They ask different people how they would like to improve the school grounds. Their questionnaire gives people a choice of four changes.

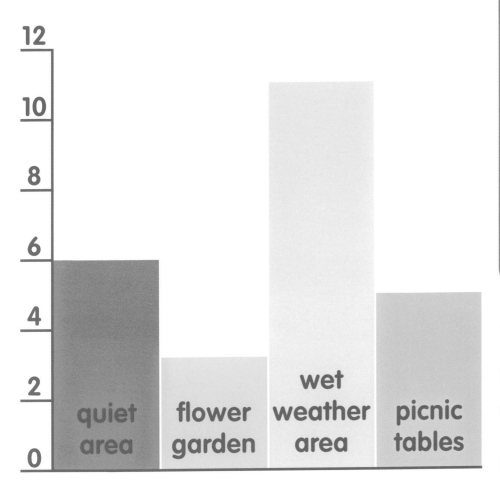

◄ Neela makes a chart showing the results. What did most people choose?

Sensory garden

Jessie and her class made a garden that appeals to the senses. They planted flowers with strong colours and smells and other plants with interesting leaves to feel.

▲ Parents helped to dig the garden.

▶ Jessie helped to plant some seeds.

appeals   senses

▲ The class made wind chimes. The chimes make
a tinkling sound when the wind blows. The children
made the chimes from old tins and lids and other
recycled materials. Why use recycled materials to
make new things?

wind chimes   recycled

Discussing and presenting

This class is **discussing** what new **equipment** they would like in their school grounds. In **circle time** when someone holds the teddy it is their turn to talk. What should everyone else do when one person is speaking?

discussing   equipment   circle time

The school decides to set up a playground committee. The committee will help to choose the playground equipment. The children decide who they want to represent them. The two children from each class with the most votes will join the committee.

▲ The children write the names on paper in secret and put them in a box.

▲ One of the class representatives presents the different choices to the whole school.

committee   represent   votes

Choices and changes

Sometimes we have to compromise. That means we have to change our choices.

◀ This playground designer is helping a school to plan a new playground. He explains that the equipment the school has chosen will not fit and would cost too much money.

What will the school have to do? How should they change their choices?

compromise   designer   explains

Does your school have **rules** about **health** and **safety**? When Li Ming's school gets a new playground the children agree a set of rules about using it.

PLAYGROUND RULES

Do not use equipment when wet.

Use play equipment properly.

No running, pushing or shoving.

No bare feet. Wear shoes.

▲ **Why do we need rules like this? How do rules help us? Which rules would you add to this list?**

Setting targets

Jack's school has set a target to raise money to improve their school grounds. They would like a new pond and garden area.

▲ Jack is writing letters to people in the locality to ask for help. Other children have helped to organise a jumble sale.

▲ A local garden shop donates some plants to the school.

target   locality   donates

Playground Toys Price List

Dodge balls	£15 each
Hoops	£20 for four
Skipping ropes	£5 each
Skittle set	£30
Coloured cones	£20 for six
Bats and balls	£20 for ten

▲ **Jack's school also raised £200 to spend on new playground toys. With this money, which toys would you choose from this price list? Remember, a school would need to buy more than one of each kind of toy.**

▲ **Some builders offer to give some time to help. These volunteers are building a wooden study area with a pond.**

volunteers   study area

Thinking about changes

Once upon a time there was a very ugly patch of land......

Look how the garden is changing

The story of our beautiful sensory garden.

Big, strong men from Treforest Day Centre come to help make our wish come true.

What will

Mr Pennell helped us become carpenters for the day

We all made a wish and drew plans of how we would like the garden to look

Improving school grounds can take a long time.

◀ This school made a **poster** to show how a patch of ground was changed into a sensory garden.

◀ It took a year to make the new sensory garden. What will the school need to do in **future** to look after the sensory garden?

poster   future

◀ These children are happy that they do not have to stay indoors when it rains at playtime. They can use their new wet weather area.

What changes has your school made? What was good about the project? What would you do differently next time?

wet weather area   differently

Further information for

Possible Activities

PAGES 4-5

Ask the children to think about how the activities in the school grounds change throughout the year. They could make a display of photos to show how the grounds change in appearance with the changing seasons. Children could find out what the most popular games in the playground are and make a chart with the results.

PAGES 6-7

Children could do some work on the history of the local environment and see how the playground has changed. Does anyone in the community have photos of what the school grounds looked like in the past? In design and technology, they could make a model of their school grounds and make changes to show what they think could be improved.

PAGES 8-9

Small-scale projects, including adding plants in container pots or making murals or playground art, are a great chance to involve members of the wider community. Add some value to a playground surface painting by making it educational as well as fun. You could show a compass, sundial or even an electric circuit. This is also a good chance to get the children involved with the idea of scale, taking a small design and scaling it up to fill a larger space in the playground.

PAGES 10-11

When interviewing people or taking surveys, an adult could video the children so that they could create a news-type broadcast about their project. Children could explore different ways of finding out what people think, such as a suggestions box. Children could also look at other ways of presenting survey results, such as pie charts.

PAGES 12-13

Instead of a sensory garden, a school could make a wildlife garden. There are lots of ideas of how to do this at http://www.bbowt.org.uk, and Learning Through Landscapes has case studies at http://www.ltl.org.uk. Timing is vital when planning any garden and this is a good chance to link with work

Parents and Teachers

on what plants need. Children could use a computer program to design a new playground. Would their design work in their own school? Do they think it would cost a lot of money?

PAGES 14-15

Having an election for a committee or voting for a change is an ideal way to introduce children to democracy. They could help make the ballot boxes and count the results. Discuss why ballots are made in secret. How many different ways of voting can you think of? People can vote online or by text, too.

PAGES 16-17

Here children could discuss negotiation and compromise. This is something they may already do in families or in class. Do children know what the school's health and safety policy is? They could design a set of rules using ideas from the health and safety policy or come up with their own. If they make a poster of rules, how can they make them persuasive and eye-catching?

PAGES 18-19

Groups of children could be given a small amount of money and, on a trip to a local nursery, choose plants for the school grounds. They could meet with a nursery gardener who could advise them on the best kinds of plants to choose.

PAGES 20-21

It is useful to make a scrapbook or timeline as a record of any school grounds project. As a literacy link, after a project has been completed children could write letters to people who helped, thanking them for their involvement and explaining the difference the change has made to them and their school. Then it is important to evaluate a project. How might it be done differently next time?

Further Information

BOOKS FOR CHILDREN

Please Play Safe! Penguin's Guide to Playground Safety by Margery Cuyler (Penguin, 2006)

Nature's Playground: Activities, Crafts and Games to Encourage Your Children to Enjoy the Great Outdoors by Fiona Danks (Frances Lincoln Publishers, 2006)

Playground Equipment (Start-Up Design and Technology series) by Louise Spilsbury (Evans Brothers, 2005)

Primary Playground Games by Cat Weatherill (Scholastic, 2003)

My New Playground (Start School series) by Jonny Zucker (Ladybird, 2005)

WEBSITES

http://www.ltl.org.uk
Learning Through Landscapes has lots of case studies and ideas for improving school grounds.

http://www.rspca.org.uk
The RSPCA site has details about how to make a wildlife garden.

http://www.eco-schools.org.uk
http://www.wwflearning.org.uk

Index